Where Did My Dog Go?

Other books by this author

WHEN GRANDMOTHER SPEAKS

Where Did My Dog Go?

Donna Sauer

Illustrations by
Heather Simons

Copyright © 2022 by Donna Sauer

All rights reserved. In accordance with the US Copyright Act of 1976, no part of this book may be reproduced by any mechanical, photographic, or electronic process; nor may it be stored in a retrieval system, transmitted, or otherwise be copied or shared for public or private use — other than for "fair use" as a brief quotation embodied in articles and reviews — without prior written permission from the publisher. For permission, contact www.drdonnaac.com

Published by Mystique of Animals Publications
For more information, visit www.drdonnaac.com

Book design by Constellation Book Services,
www.constellationbookservices.com

ISBN (hardcover): ISBN 978-0-578-28608-2

Printed in the United States of America

This book is dedicated to Angel and
all our beloved pets who have crossed
over the rainbow bridge.

She sensed the rhythmic ebb and flow
in the breath of the world
and practiced that breathing
with the intensity of the now
in all that is.

Preface

For a child whose pet has died, this book is meant to bring them comfort and assure them they are not to blame by word or thought for theIr companion animal's death. The illustrations and text convey a view of never-ending love between the child and pet and is designed to bring the child freeing happiness from grief, allowing expression of gratitude for wonderful times shared.

Note: Parents, you may wish to substitute the name of your child's pet for the word "dog" as you read this book to your child.

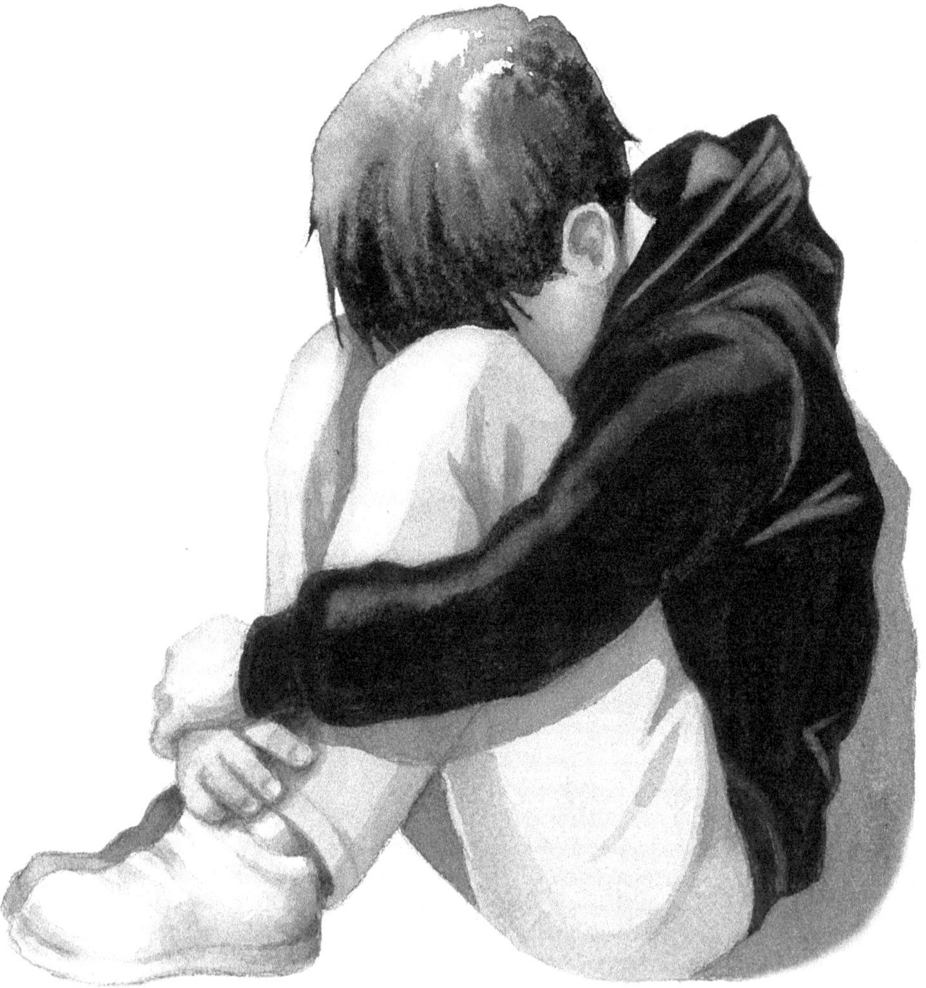

Do you feel sad your dog has gone away from you?

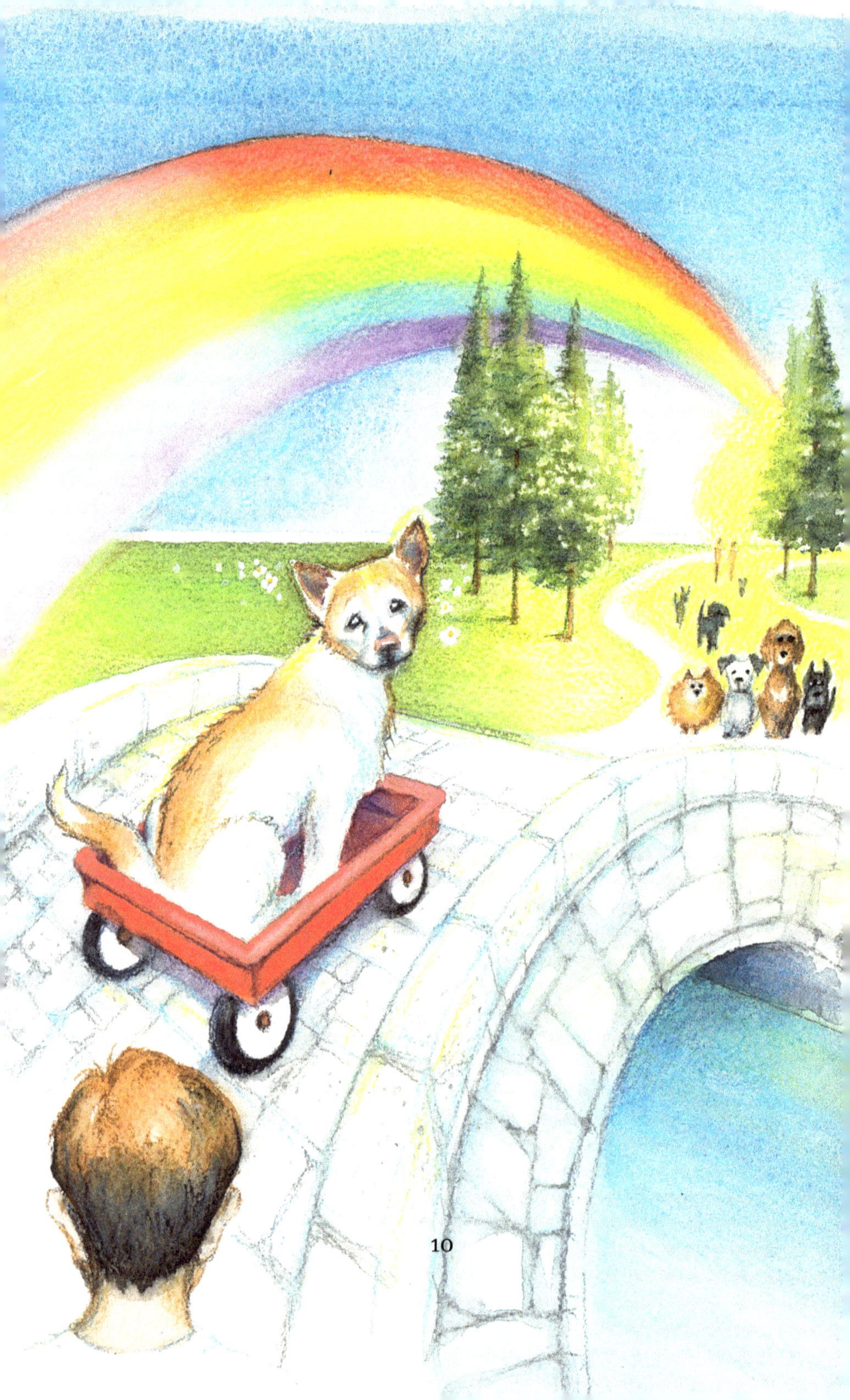

If your dog has died and crossed over the rainbow bridge to be with the angels, do you wish with all your heart you could have him with you again?

12

Your dog is a loving being who came for a time to share with you and love and help you. But he could not stay forever as the warm furry body you cuddled and hugged.

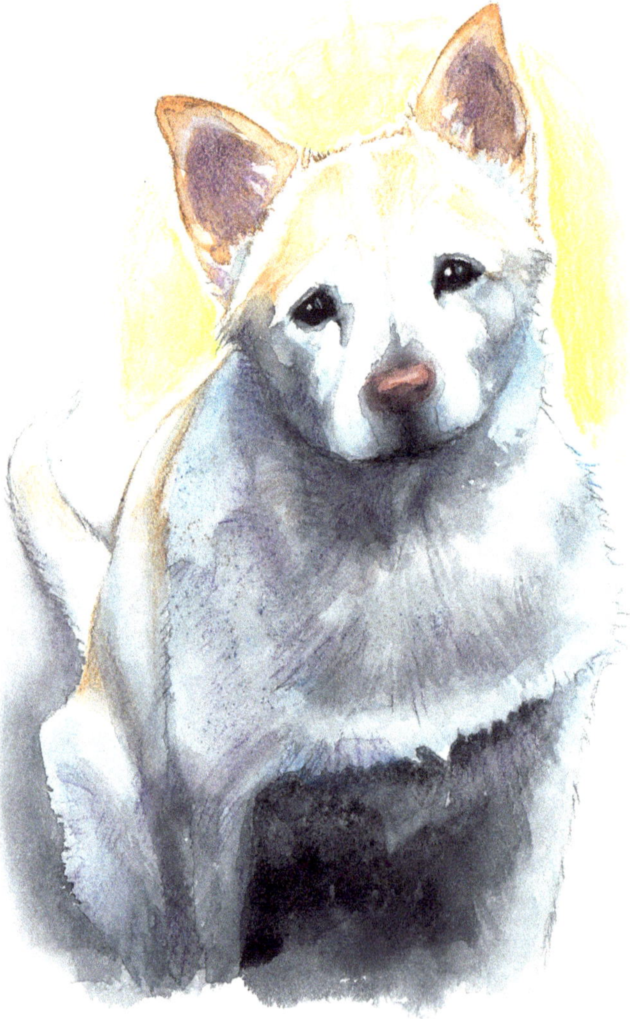

Yet lovingly your dog is still with you. His angel spirit surrounds you with love and protection and quiet peace. He wants you to be happy.

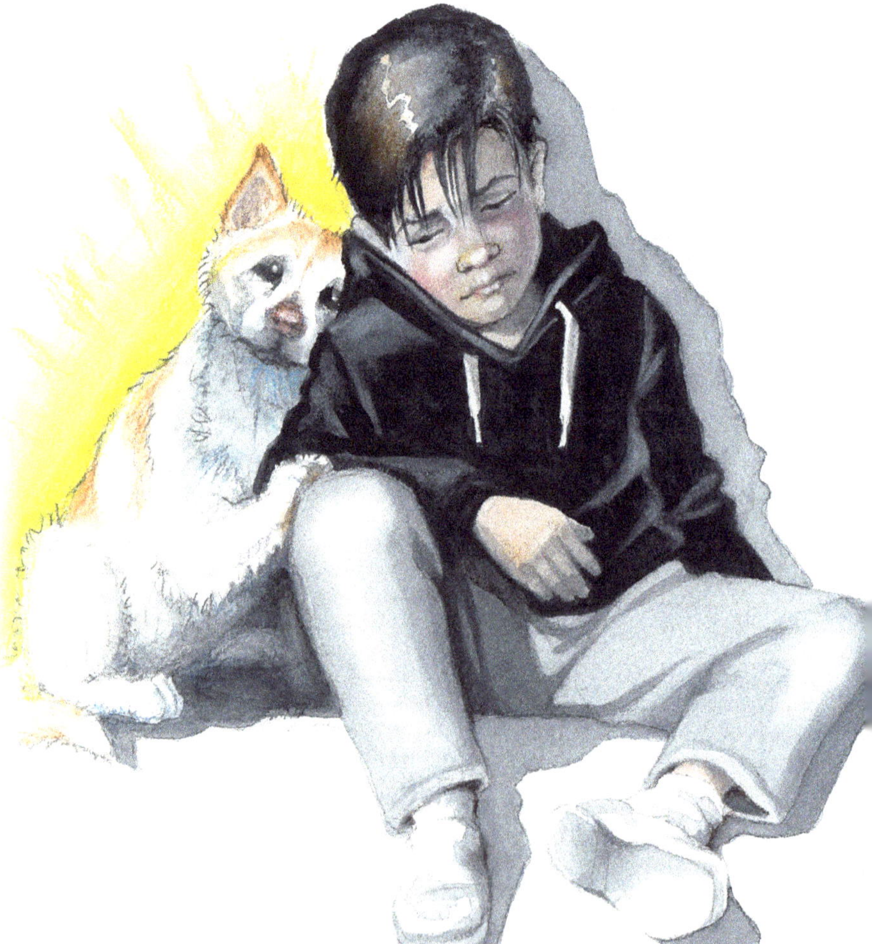

Do you cry and feel sad your pet is gone? Then know he is there right beside you, tail wagging, licking away your tears, paw on your arm, comforting you.

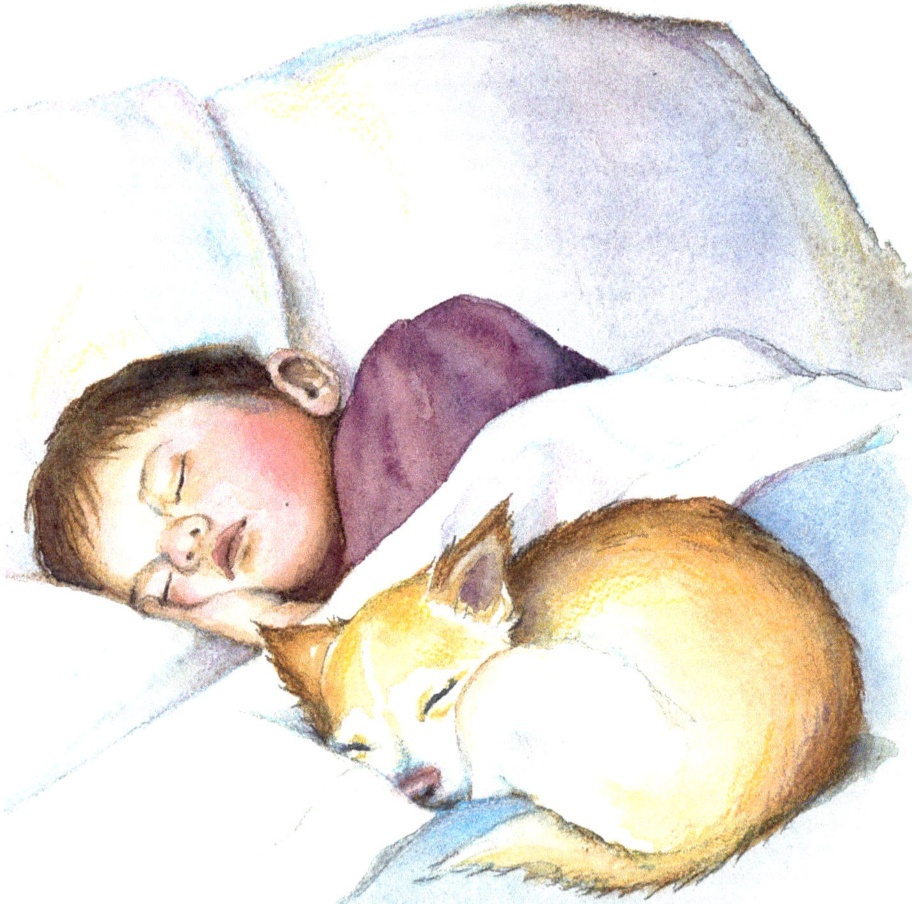

Do you fall asleep at night and imagine your dog is in your bed, nestled next to your chest? Then, of course, he is there beside you, quietly snoring, just as he used to do, bringing you peace and calm.

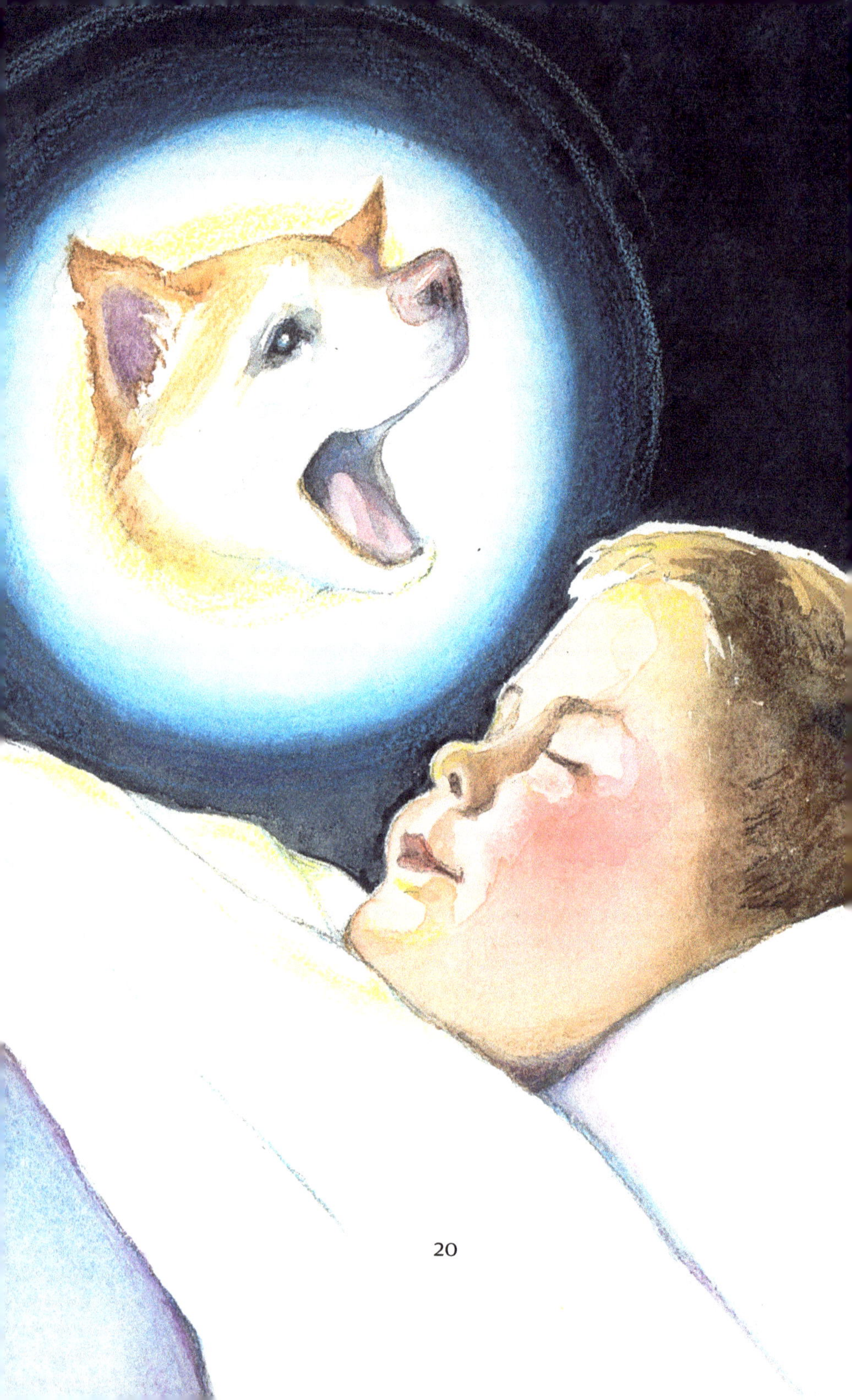

Have you seen your dog in your dreams? Have you heard a familiar bark you know so well? Yes, he is letting you know he is still loves you.

22

Do you imagine your dog flying free and healthy now and running through the billowy white clouds in a blue sky? Then he is sitting beside you, asking you look up and see him, showing you his beautiful face in the sky.

24

Did you make a little remembering place for your dog with his picture and perhaps a favorite toy? Well then, each time you see his picture, he is at once with you, wanting you to know he will never forget you either.

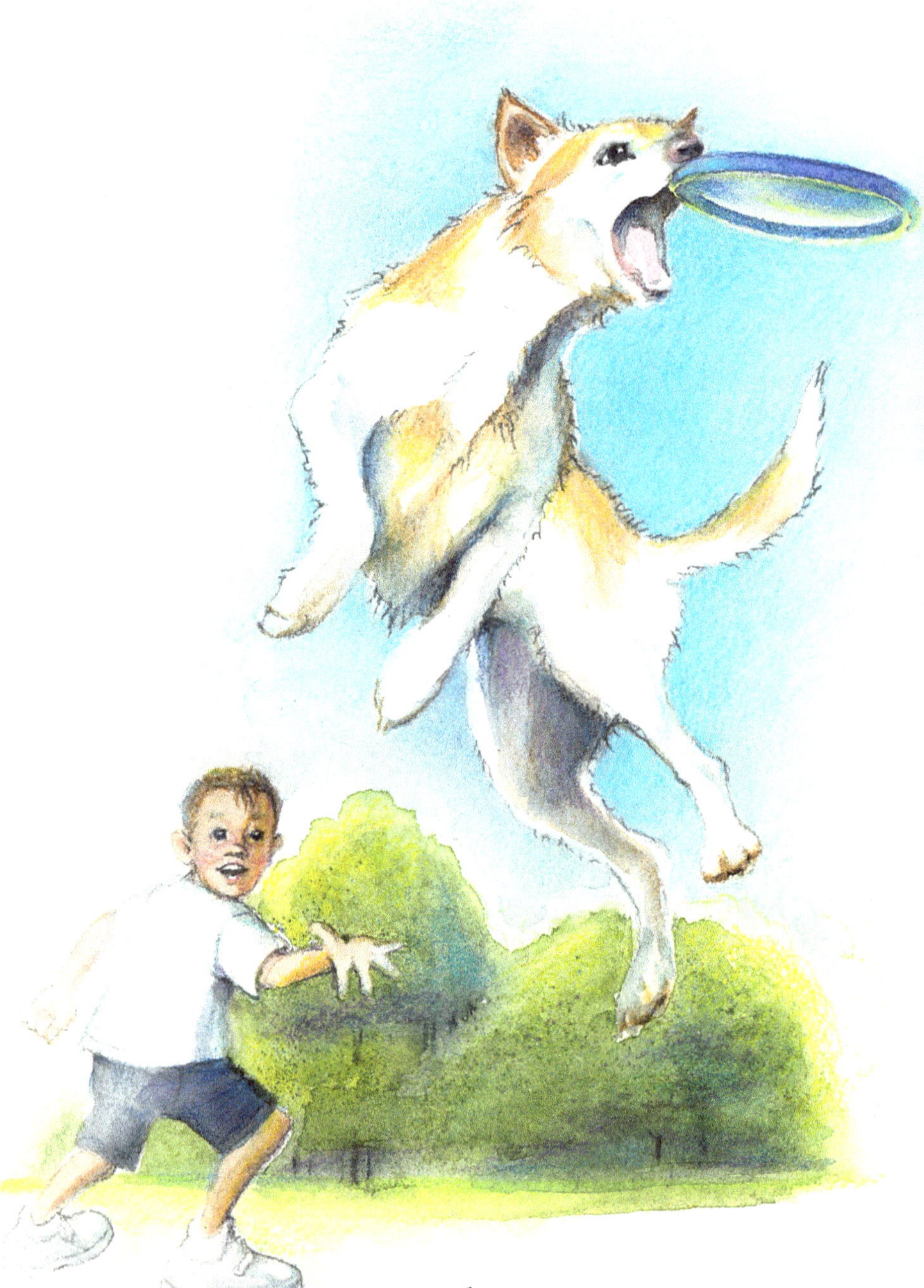

Your dog will forever be with you. When you grow older and remember the happy times you played with him, how you laughed at his funny, goofy self, he will be there, frisbee in mouth, tail wagging, showing you so many wonderful moments you shared.

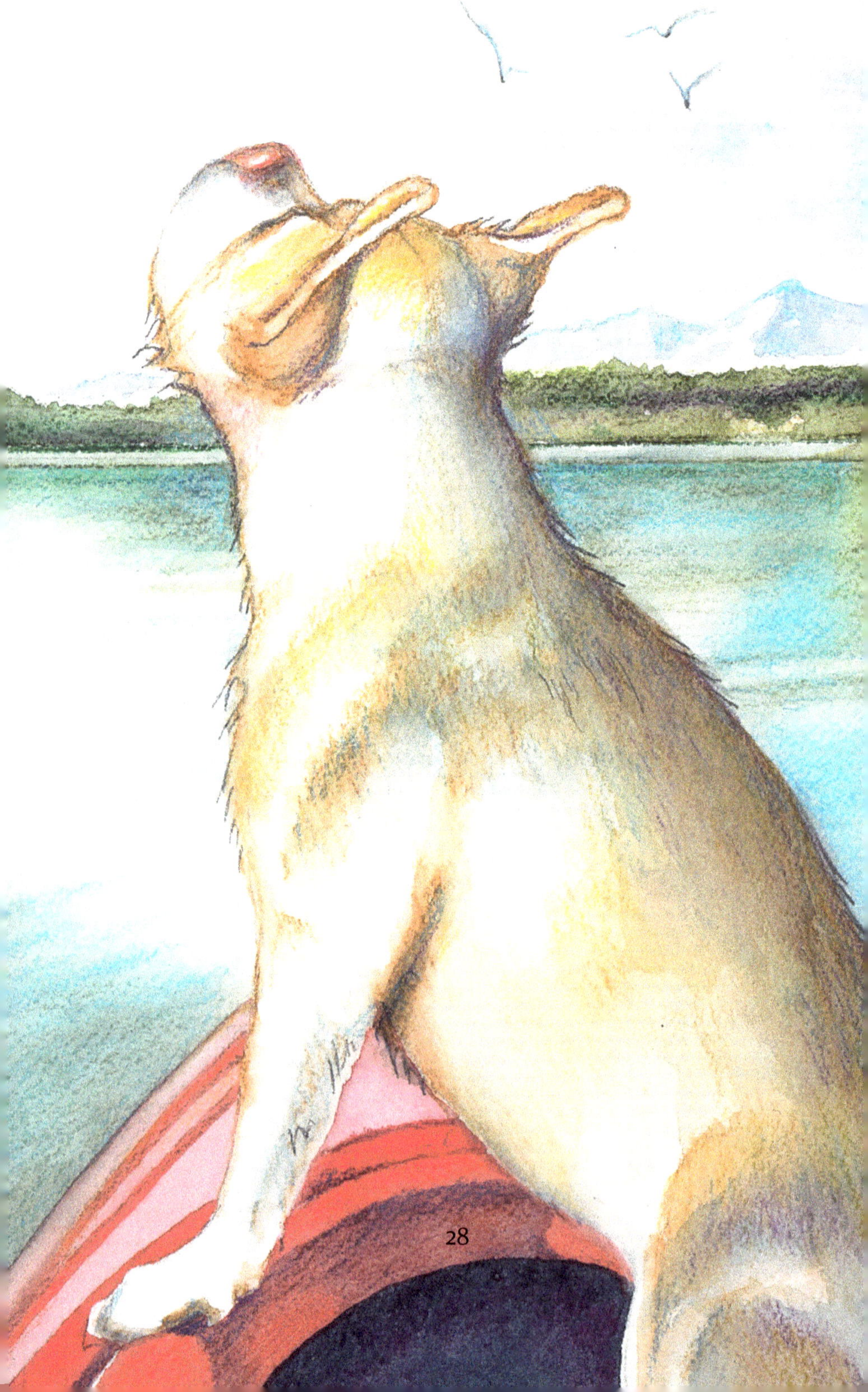

Perhaps when you are older, you will be in a kayak, enjoying the sun and water, and will think how much your dog would have loved being there with you. And for sure, he will be standing tall on the front of the boat, nose pointed into the wind, ear flapping, enjoying that very moment with you.

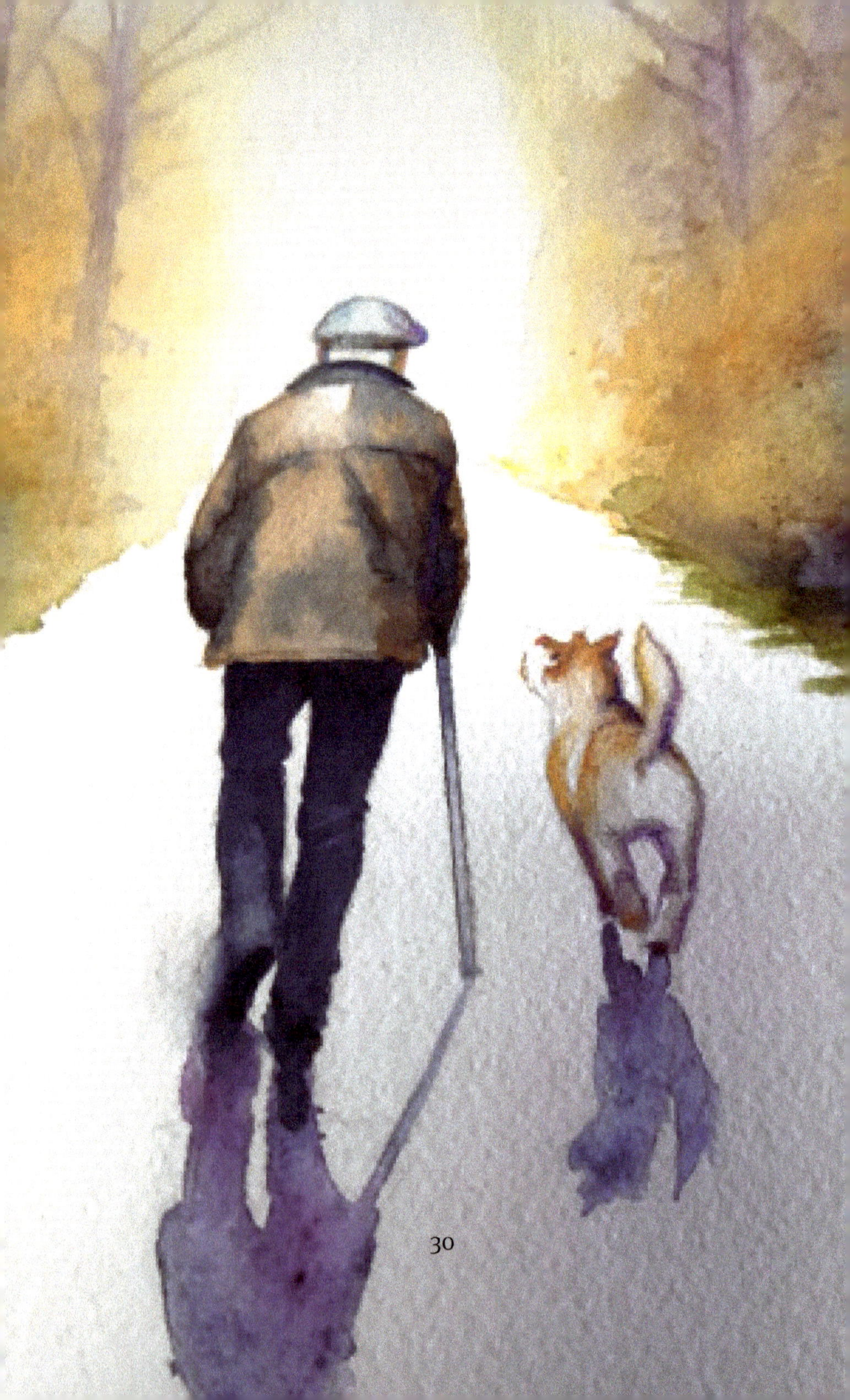

And when you are very old and your body is tired, your dog will come and walk with you, helping you to be strong and happy.
He will remind you he will forever be beside you.

32

Where did your dog go? He went everywhere all at once. Do not be sad. Be grateful for the happy and loving times together. Look for him. He is with you for always in so many ways, bringing joy and comfort. When you think of him, he is there. When you sleep, he is there. When you are sad, he is there. For love shared is the most precious thing and it never ends.

About the Author

Dr. Donna Sauer has a master's degree in Zoology as well as a PhD in biology. After many years of teaching sciences at the college level, she now directs her life work towards Animal Communication and Energy Healing. She is a graduate of the Lynn McKenzie Animal Energy Communication Institute and also a Reiki Master and follower of Lakota Healing Traditions.

She resides in Washington State on a small farm which she shares with rescue animals and a plethora of trees and flowers, all of which delight, teach and energize her each and every day.

Her animal communication readings and energy healing session keep her busy along with writings and teaching animal communication skills. At the heart of her work is a wish to help each unique being come into the full potential of their divine life path within the universality of unconditional love and acceptance.

Contact information:

Dr. Donna Sauer
Animal Energy Healer and Communicator
www.drdonnaac.com

J. Belle Photography
www.pixbyjenn.zenfolio.com

CPSIA information can be obtained
at www.ICGtesting.com
Printed in the USA
BVHW022020100722
641786BV00005B/47